Merry Christmas!

Thank you for giving of your time and talents to our small group program. If you've never kept a journal before, I hope you will give this a try. One suggestion to consider would be a prayer journal. Remember to go back and write how God answered your prayer. May God bless you with a happy, healthy 2023!

This book belongs to:

Bill

from Jane Roseberry

God is... therefore, I am...

Taste and see that the LORD is good; blessed is the one who takes refuge in him.

Psalm 34:8

Even though I walk through the darkest valley, I will fear no evil, for you are with me; your rod and your staff, they comfort me.

The righteous person may have many troubles, but the LORD delivers him from them all;

Psalm 34:19

Take delight in the LORD, and he will give you the desires of your heart.

Psalm 37:4

Cast your cares on the LORD and he will sustain you; he will never let the righteous be shaken.

Psalm 55:22

Your word is a lamp for my feet, a light on my path.
Psalm 119:105

My help comes from the LORD, the Maker of heaven and earth.
Psalm 121:2

Commit to the LORD whatever you do, and he will establish your plans.

Proverbs 16:3

The name of the LORD is a fortified tower; the righteous run to it and are safe.

Proverbs 18:10

For I know the plans I have for you," declares the LORD, "plans to prosper you and not to harm you, plans to give you hope and a future.
Jeremiah 29:11

*Come to me, all you who are weary and burdened,
and I will give you rest.*

Matthew 11:28

And we know that in all things God works for the good of those who love him who have been called according to his purpose.
Romans 8:28

Because he himself suffered when he was tempted, he is able to help those who are being tempted.

Hebrews 2:18

Cast all your anxiety on him because he cares for you.
1 Peter 5:7

You, dear children, are from God and have overcome them, because the one who is in you is greater than the one who is in the world.

1 John 4:4

Be strong and courageous. Do not be afraid or terrified because of them, for the LORD your God goes with you; he will never leave you nor forsake you."

Deuteronomy 31:6

The LORD himself goes before you and will be with you; he will never leave you nor forsake you. Do not be afraid; do not be discouraged."

Deuteronomy 31:8

Have I not commanded you? Be strong and courageous. Do not be terrified; do not be discouraged, for the LORD your God will be with you wherever you go.
Joshua 1:9

Joshua said to them, "Do not be afraid; do not be discouraged. Be strong and courageous. This is what the LORD will do to all the enemies you are going to fight."

Joshua 10:25

The LORD is a refuge for the oppressed, a stronghold in times of trouble.
Psalm 9:9

I keep my eyes always on the LORD. With him at my right hand, I will not be shaken.

Psalm 16:8

Wait for the LORD; be strong and take heart and wait for the LORD.

Psalm 27:14

Since you are my rock and my fortress, for the sake of your name lead and guide me.

Psalm 31:3

I will instruct you and teach you in the way you should go; I will counsel you with my loving eye on you.

Psalm 32:8

The LORD will rescue his servants; no one who takes refuge in him will be condemned.

Psalm 34:22

Take delight in the LORD, and he will give you the desires of your heart.
Psalm 37:4

Cast your cares on the LORD and he will sustain you; he will never let the righteous be shaken.

Psalm 55:22

Truly he is my rock and my salvation; he is my fortress, I will not be shaken.

Psalm 62:6

The LORD is my strength and my defense; he has become my salvation.

Psalm 118:14

*You are my refuge and my shield; I have put my hope in your word.
Away from me, you evildoers, that I may keep the commands of my God!*
Psalm 119:114-115

I am laid low in the dust; preserve my life according to your word!
Psalm 119:25

My comfort in my suffering is this: Your promise preserves my life.
Psalm 119:50

It was good for me to be afflicted so that I might learn your decrees.
Psalm 119:71

I call on the LORD in my distress, and he answers me.
Psalm 120:1

The LORD will keep you from all harm—he will watch over your life;
Psalm 121:7

The LORD will watch over your coming and going both now and forevermore.

Psalm 121:8

The LORD is near to all who call on him, to all who call on him in truth.
Psalm 145:18

*He fulfills the desires of those who fear him; he
hears their cry and saves them.*
Psalm 145:19

He holds success in store for the upright, he is a shield to those whose walk is blameless.
Proverbs 2:7

Trust in the LORD with all your heart and lean not on your own understanding; in all your ways submit to him, and he will make your paths straight.
Proverbs 3:5-6

A generous person will prosper; whoever refreshes others will be refreshed.
Proverbs 11:25

Commit to the LORD whatever you do, and he will establish your plans.
Proverbs 16:3

A friend loves at all times, and a brother is born for a time of adversity.
Proverbs 17:17

*The name of the LORD is a fortified tower; the
righteous run to it and are safe.*
Proverbs 18:10

You will keep in perfect peace those whose minds are
steadfast, because they trust in you.
Isaiah 26:3

People of Zion, who live in Jerusalem, you will weep no more. How gracious he will be when you cry for help! As soon as he hears, he will answer you.
Isaiah 30:19

For I am the LORD your God who takes hold of your right hand and says to you, Do not fear; I will help you.

Isaiah 41:13

But those who hope in the LORD will renew their strength. They will soar on wings like eagles; they will run and not grow weary, they will walk and not be faint.
Isaiah 40:31

So do not fear, for I am with you; do not be dismayed, for I am your God. I will strengthen you and help you; I will uphold you with my righteous right hand.

Isaiah 41:10

But now, this is what the LORD says—he who created you, O Jacob, he who formed you, O Israel: "Fear not, for I have redeemed you; I have summoned you by name; you are mine.

Isaiah 43:1

No weapon forged against you will prevail, and you will refute every tongue that accuses you. This is the heritage of the servants of the LORD, and this is their vindication from me," declares the LORD.
Isaiah 54:17

The LORD is good to those whose hope is in him, to the one who seeks him
Lamentations 3:25

For I know the plans I have for you," declares the LORD, "plans to prosper you and not to harm you, plans to give you hope and a future.

Jeremiah 29:11

The LORD is good, a refuge in times of trouble. He cares for those who trust in him.

Nahum 1:7

But seek first his kingdom and his righteousness, and all these things will be given to you as well.
Matthew 6:33

*Come to me, all you who are weary and burdened,
and I will give you rest.*

Matthew 11:28

*I have given you authority to trample on snakes and scorpions and
to overcome all the power of the enemy; nothing will harm you.*
Luke 10:19

For God so loved the world that he gave his one and only Son, that whoever believes in him shall not perish but have eternal life.

John 3:16

Very truly I tell you, the one who believes has eternal life.
John 6:47

Peace I leave with you; my peace I give you. I do not give to you as the world gives. Do not let your hearts be troubled and do not be afraid.
John 14:27

Remain in me, as I also remain in you. No branch can bear fruit by itself; it must remain in the vine. Neither can you bear fruit unless you remain in me.

John 15:4

Greater love has no one than this: to lay down one's life for one's friends.

John 15:13

I have told you these things, so that in me you may have peace. In this world you will have trouble. But take heart! I have overcome the world.

John 16:33

But thanks be to God! He gives us the victory through our Lord Jesus Christ.

1 Corinthians 15:57

Be on your guard; stand firm in the faith; be courageous; be strong.

1 Corinthians 16:13

Now thanks be to God who always leads us in triumph in Christ.

2 Corinthians 2:14

We are hard pressed on every side, but not crushed; perplexed, but not in despair; persecuted, but not abandoned; struck down, but not destroyed.

2 Corinthians 4:8-9

For we live by faith, not by sight.
2 Corinthians 5:7

Therefore, if anyone is in Christ, the new creation has come: The old has gone, the new is here!

2 Corinthians 5:17

The mind governed by the flesh is death, but the mind governed by the Spirit is life and peace.

Romans 8:6

And we know that in all things God works for the good of those who love him who have been called according to his purpose.

Romans 8:28

What, then, shall we say in response to these things? If God is for us, who can be against us?
Romans 8:31

For everything that was written in the past was written to teach us, so that through the endurance taught in the Scriptures and the encouragement they provide we might have hope.

Romans 15:4

Finally, be strong in the Lord and in his mighty power.
Ephesians 6:10

And my God will meet all your needs according to the riches of his glory in Christ Jesus.

Philippians 4:19

Let the peace of Christ rule in your hearts, since as members of one body you were called to peace. And be thankful.

Colossians 3:15

But the Lord is faithful, and he will strengthen and protect you from the evil one.

2 Thessalonians 3:3

For the Spirit God gave us does not make us timid, but gives us power, love and self-discipline.

2 Timothy 1:7

The Lord will rescue me from every evil attack and will bring me safely to his heavenly kingdom. To him be glory for ever and ever. Amen.

2 Timothy 4:18

Because he himself suffered when he was tempted, he is able to help those who are being tempted.

Hebrews 2:18

*But Christ is faithful as the Son over God's house. And we are his house,
if indeed we hold firmly to our confidence and the hope in which we glory.*
Hebrews 3:6

Keep your lives free from the love of money and be content with what you have, because God has said, "Never will I leave you; never will I forsake you."

Hebrews 13:5

Cast all your anxiety on him because he cares for you.
1 Peter 5:7

*You, dear children, are from God and have overcome them, because
the one who is in you is greater than the one who is in the world.*

1 John 4:4

There is no fear in love. But perfect love drives out fear, because fear has to do with punishment. The one who fears is not made perfect in love.

1 John 4:18

This calls for patient endurance on the part of the people of God who keep his commands and remain faithful to Jesus.

Revelation 14:12

The blessing of the Lord brings wealth, and he adds no trouble to it.
Proverbs 10:22

Blessed is the man who makes the Lord his trust, who does not look to the proud, to those who turn aside to false gods.

Psalm 40:4

The LORD is my light and my salvation; whom shall I fear? The LORD is the strength of my life; of whom shall I be afraid?

Psalm 27:1

But the salvation of the righteous is from the LORD; He is their strength in time of trouble.

Psalm 37:39

But Jesus looked at them and said to them, 'With men this is impossible, but with God all things are possible.

Matthew 19:26

I can do all things through Christ who strengthens me.
Philippians 4:13

For God has not given us a spirit of fear, but of power and of love and of a sound mind.

2 Timothy 1:7

It is God who arms me with strength, and makes my way perfect.

Psalm 18:32

Let the words of my mouth and the meditation of my heart be acceptable in Your sight, O LORD, my strength and my Redeemer.

Psalm 19:14

But You, O LORD, do not be far from Me; O My Strength, hasten to help Me!

Psalm 22:19

The LORD will give strength to His people; the LORD will bless His people with peace.

Psalm 29:11

The LORD is my strength and song, and He has become my salvation.
Psalm 118:14

For You have been a strength to the poor, a strength to the needy in his distress, a refuge from the storm, a shade from the heat; for the blast of the terrible ones is as a storm against the wall.
Isaiah 25:4

Seek the LORD and His strength; seek His face evermore!
1 Chronicles 16:11

The God of my strength, in whom I will trust; my shield and the horn of my salvation, my stronghold and my refuge; my Savior, You save me from violence.

2 Samuel 22:3

Fear not, for I am with you; be not dismayed, for I am your God. I will strengthen you, yes, I will help you, I will uphold you with My righteous right hand.

Isaiah 41:10

Ah, Lord GOD! Behold, You have made the heavens and the earth by Your great power and outstretched arm. There is nothing too hard for You.

Jeremiah 32:17

He heals the brokenhearted and binds up their wounds.

Psalm 147:3

The LORD God is my strength; He will make my feet like deer's feet, and He will make me walk on my high hills.

Habakkuk 3:19

Not by might nor by power, but by My Spirit,' says the LORD of hosts.
Zechariah 4:6

Now to Him who is able to do exceedingly abundantly above all that we ask or think, according to the power that works in us, to Him be the glory in the church by Christ Jesus to all generations, forever and ever. Amen.
Ephesians 3:20-21

Finally, my brethren, be strong in the Lord and in the power of His might.
Ephesians 6:10

Made in the USA
Las Vegas, NV
28 September 2022